For and Agai

by Jenny Alexander

Contents

Longman

Edinburgh Gate
Harlow, Essex

For and Against ... *Having to Earn your Pocket Money*

Most parents give their children pocket money every week, but some parents expect them to work for it. Is this a good idea?

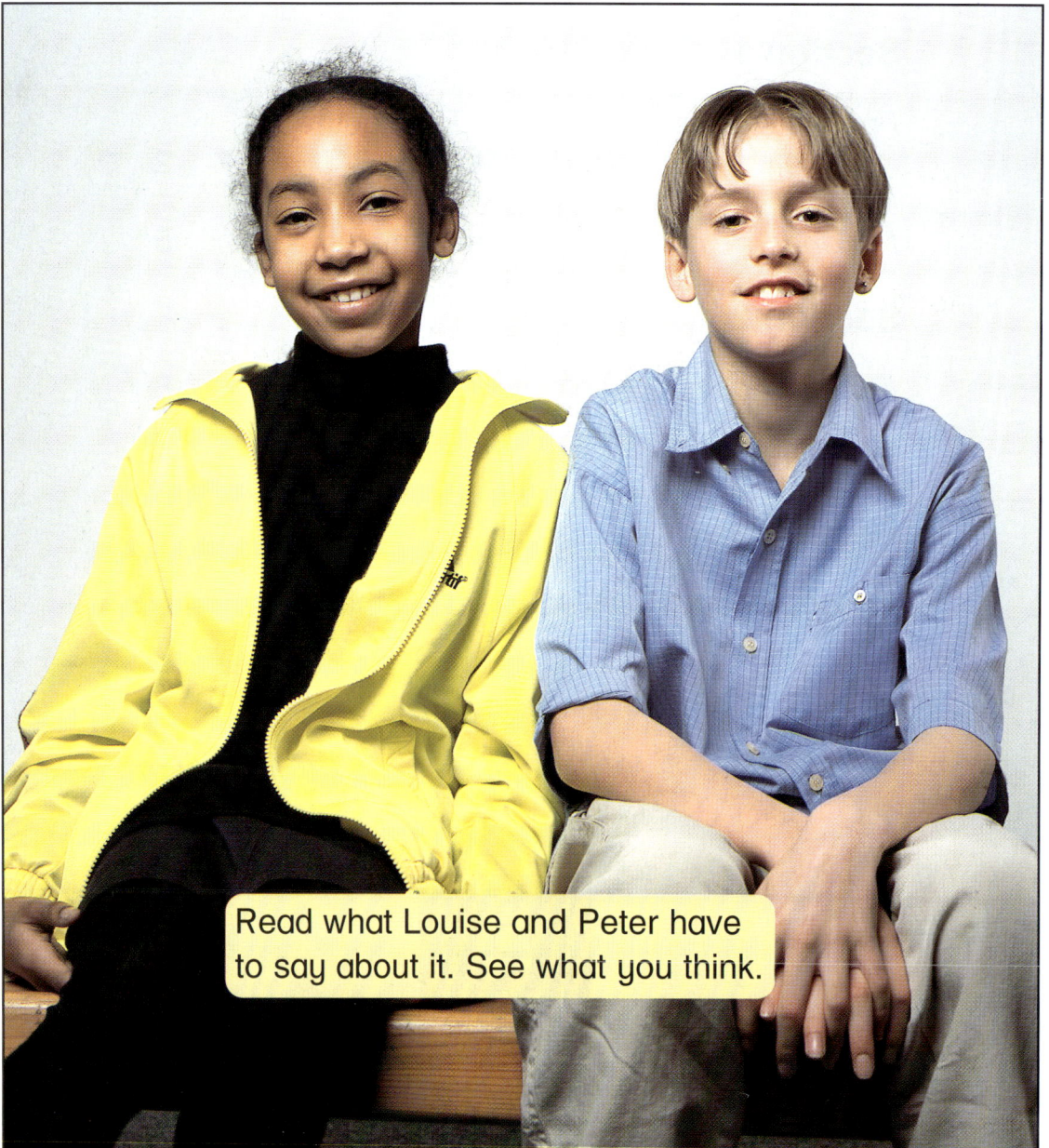

Read what Louise and Peter have to say about it. See what you think.

For Earning your Pocket Money

My name is Louise Johnson. I am nine years old. I have two brothers, aged eight and eleven. We have to earn our pocket money by helping with the housework.

I think working for your pocket money helps you to feel more grown up. It means your parents notice all the jobs you do. It's a way for them to say, 'Thank-you for helping!'

We don't argue very much about who does the work in our house. My brothers and I are usually keen to do our chores because we want to get as much money as possible.

Sometimes I get in a bad mood and I don't want to do my work. Then I just leave it. I don't have to feel guilty because I know it's up to me – no work, no money!

Working for your pocket money teaches you to be more careful about how you spend it. If I see something I want in a shop, I think, 'I would have to wash up every day for a week to buy that. Is it worth it?'

The other thing we have to do to earn our pocket money is keep up with our homework. It's just as well, because I hate doing homework! Sometimes, knowing I will only get all my pocket money if I do it is the only thing that keeps me going.

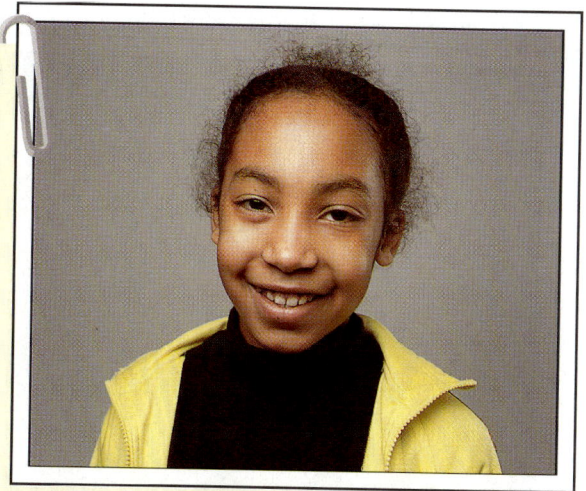

Against Earning your Pocket Money

My name is Peter Ryan. I am nine years old, and I have a big sister aged thirteen. We have to help around the house, but we don't have to earn our pocket money. We get that anyway, whatever we do.

Some people say it's more grown up to get paid for the work you do, but my Mum and Dad don't get paid for doing the washing-up and hoovering. They do it for the sake of the family.

I like to think that I am helping my parents when I do my chores. If I got money for everything I did, I would feel I was just helping myself.

We do argue quite a bit about how we share out the work in our house, but I don't see a problem with that. I think it's good to learn how to fight your corner and get a fair deal. It's good to learn when you have to back down, too!

Some of my friends only get their pocket money if they do their homework. I think that isn't fair, because it gives their parents too much power. I am glad my parents leave my homework up to me.

I think of my pocket money as a present. My parents give it to me because they love me. If they gave it to me for doing work, I don't think it would feel so good.

For and Against ... *School Uniform*

Most children in British schools have to wear school uniform. Some people love it, other people hate it. Here are some of the arguments for and against school uniform:

For	Against
School uniform looks smart	**School uniform looks boring**
School uniform makes children look smart, and that makes the whole school look better. Then children feel proud of their school.	School uniform makes children look boring, and that makes the whole school look boring too. Then children feel bored with school.

For	Against

For

Wearing uniform makes children behave well

Children who are proud of their school behave well **outside school** because they don't want to let the school down. Also, if they did something bad outside school, everyone could tell which school they came from, so they would be more likely to get caught.

School uniform helps children behave well **inside school**, because it teaches them to do as they are told.

It makes children behave better **at home**, because they can't argue with their parents about what they are going to wear.

Against

Wearing uniform makes children behave badly

Children who are bored with school behave badly to liven things up. Wearing uniform means they can behave badly **outside school** because they all look the same, so no-one can tell who they are.

Inside school, having to wear uniform makes children rebel, because it is hard to obey rules you can't see any reason for.

Teachers have to waste time making sure everyone's got the right sweatshirt on, when they could be dealing with more important things like good manners.

School uniform makes it easier to steal other people's clothes without being caught, because they all look the same.

At home, children are more likely to argue with their parents because they can't see why they have to wear a uniform when most parents don't.

For	Against
School uniform is a good thing for poor people	**School uniform is a bad thing for poor people**
School uniform means you can't tell who is rich and who is poor because it makes everyone look the same.	You can always tell who is rich and who is poor because you have to wear the same clothes all the time, and they soon look old and tatty. Only the richer people can afford to keep buying new ones.
It is cheaper to buy than other clothes because there are no **designer labels**.	School uniform means you have to buy lots of clothes in one go when you start a new school.
	Good second-hand uniforms are hard to come by because children wear them every day and they get worn out.

Because people either love school uniform or hate it, some schools are trying a new idea. They are letting their pupils choose whether to wear school uniform or not.

It will be interesting to see what most children decide.

For and Against ...Television

It's hard to imagine life without **television**. But a lot of
older people can remember a time when there was
no television, and some say that life was better then.
So is television a good thing?

For Television

Most people must think that television is a good thing, because most people choose to have one. The main reason is probably just that television makes life more interesting. But there are lots of others ...

1 **Television is good for your health**

Watching television at the end of a stressful day is a great way of relaxing. Funny programmes that make you laugh are particularly good for you, because laughter is a tonic and it helps to keep you healthy.

2 **Television is good for your family life**

Watching television is something that people of all ages can enjoy doing together. It gives you lots of things to talk about. It also helps at times when you don't want to be together, like when you're tired and grumpy after school. Then you can go off and watch television on your own instead of getting into arguments.

3 **Television is good for your social life**

Television programmes give you ideas for games to play with your friends. Seeing how people sort out their problems in **soaps** and dramas can help you to understand other people's problems and sort out your own.

4 Television is educational

On television, you can see places, animals and people you would never see in normal, everyday life. Watching television is better than learning from books because a book leaves too much to the imagination.

Against Television

The main argument against television is that it is addictive. The more you watch, the more you want to watch, and the harder it gets to turn it off. But there are lots of others ...

1 **Television can be bad for your health**

When you are watching television you are indoors, instead of being outside getting lots of fresh air, sunshine and exercise. Also, the adverts on television make you want to eat too many snacks.

2 **Television can be bad for family life**

Watching television stops you talking to each other. It means you have less time for playing games together or going out. It often causes arguments over which channel to watch. Sometimes there will be three or four family members alone in different rooms watching different televisions.

3 Television can be bad for your social life

Gloomy and frightening programmes can make you feel anxious about other people. Adverts and programmes about happy successful people can make you feel bad about yourself, if you feel you don't measure up.

4 Television is not as educational as people think

Even **documentaries** and the news can be misleading, because they can only show some of the facts, and not all of them. Then viewers feel they are getting the whole picture, when they are really only seeing what the programme-makers choose to show them. Books are a better way of learning because you have to use your imagination, which is much more enjoyable.

Conclusion

Television is a good servant and a bad master – that is to say, it's great if you don't let it take over.

All the problems with television can be solved if you:

- choose programmes that interest you and make you feel good

- don't assume that everything you see is true

- switch off when there's nothing worth watching.

For and Against ... *Cycling to School*

In the old days a lot of children used to cycle to school because very few families had a car. Nowadays a lot of families have a car, and very few children cycle to school.

With the roads getting more crowded all the time, and children getting less fit, some people would like to see children start cycling to school again. But would that be a good idea?

For Cycling to School

Cycling to school is good for **children**, **families**, **schools** and the **environment**.

Cycling to school is good for children because:

- it helps them to keep fit

- it helps them to learn, because exercise is good for the brain

- it helps them to feel happy – doctors have found that exercise is better than tablets for getting rid of stress and unhappiness

- cycling means children don't have to wait around for buses or lifts

- it allows them to be more independent

- it helps children develop the skills and confidence to use their bikes for other things, like visiting friends and going to the shops.

Children cycling to school is good for families because:

- it doesn't cost anything

- it means parents don't have to do the 'school run'.

Children cycling to school is good for schools because:

🚴 exercise refreshes the brain – so children who cycle arrive at school more alert and ready to learn

🚴 fewer cars and buses outside school means fewer parking problems

🚴 fewer cars and buses outside school also means roads and car parks near schools are safer for people arriving and leaving on foot.

Cycling to school is good for the environment because:

🚴 it doesn't use any fuel

🚴 it doesn't cause any pollution

🚴 it eases traffic problems – in some areas, 40% of cars on the road between eight and nine o'clock in the morning are driven by parents taking their children to school.

All these are good reasons for cycling to school, but there are also good reasons against it.

Against Cycling to School

Cycling to school is bad for **children**, **families**, and **schools**.

It is bad for children because:

- there is a risk of accidents

- cycling is tiring

- it is difficult to carry heavy school bags on a bike

- it is stressful cycling on busy roads

- in rainy weather children who cycle arrive at school wet and muddy

- cycling can be lonely – you can't chat with friends on a bike, as you could in a car or walking to a bus-stop and travelling on a bus.

Cycling to school is bad for families because:

🚲 it means parents miss the chance to talk to their children in the car

🚲 parents come to school less often, so they don't get to know other parents so well, or meet the teachers

🚲 it costs money to buy a bike, a cycle helmet and so on

🚲 it takes time and effort to maintain a bike

🚲 a lot of parents worry about children having an accident when they are out on their bikes.

It is bad for schools because:

🚲 they have to provide bike sheds

🚲 they have to sort things out when bikes are damaged or stolen at school

🚲 children who cycle can arrive at school feeling tired

🚲 cycling means children come to school wet on wet days, cold on cold days, and hot on hot days.

Conclusion

> There are lots of reasons why cycling to school is good for children, families and the environment. These reasons have not changed since the old days. Another thing that has not changed is that most children still enjoy cycling.

> To see why children don't cycle to school so much now, we need to look at the arguments against it. The big change here is that cycling is far less safe than it used to be. What do you think could be done to make it safer?

For and Against ... *Always Telling the Truth*

Most people say you should always tell the truth.
"Honesty is the best policy," they say.

The main argument for telling the truth is that if you always do so, other people will be able to trust you. But on the other hand, if you always have to tell the truth, how could anybody trust you to keep a secret ?

Is honesty always the best policy?

For Always Telling the Truth

Here are some good reasons for always telling the truth:

1 If you always tell the truth, other people will always believe you. Otherwise, you will be like the boy who cried "Wolf!"

Once a shepherd boy was guarding his flock when he thought he saw a wolf. He cried out in alarm, "Wolf! Wolf!" and all the villagers ran to help him chase the wolf away. The boy was mistaken – there wasn't any wolf. But he thought it was such a great way to make everyone take notice of him, that he took to crying "Wolf!" whenever he got bored. The first few times, the villagers came running. But then they realised he was lying, so they stopped believing him. One day, a wolf really came. The boy cried "Wolf!" but nobody took any notice.

2 You should tell the truth because other people can feel hurt or angry if they find out you have lied to them. Telling lies can get you in trouble with teachers and other grown-ups, and upset your friends.

3 You should tell the truth because it makes life simpler. When you tell lies it can be hard to remember exactly what you said, and you never know when you might give yourself away.

4 You should always tell the truth because one lie leads to another.

5 Telling the truth is the right thing to do, so if you always tell the truth you will feel good about yourself.

Against Always Telling the Truth

Here are some good reasons why honesty is not always the best policy:

1 Sometimes telling the truth would be bad manners. For example, calling people fat or ugly – even if they are – is not polite.

2 If you always tell the truth, you can hurt people's feelings. For example, if a friend asks you over and you don't want to go, it would be less hurtful to say, "I'd love to, but I'm afraid I've got something else on," than, "No thanks. I don't want to."

3 Telling the truth can sometimes be tactless. It would not be a good idea to tell your mum that you didn't like her new hairstyle, for instance, if she had just spent the afternoon at the hairdresser's.

4 If you always have to tell the truth you can never promise to keep a secret. Sometimes you can only be loyal to a friend if you lie, or pretend you don't know.

5 Sometimes telling the truth can get someone else into trouble. Supposing you see one boy hit another in the playground, for example, but you know he was being provoked. You might not want him to get told off by a teacher who doesn't know the whole story.

6 Telling the truth can get you into trouble, too. For example, is your teacher going to be happier with an excuse like, "I didn't do my homework because I didn't have time," or with the truth, "I couldn't be bothered"?

7 If you always tell the truth about what you are thinking and feeling, it can make you vulnerable. Parents and teachers say, "Pretend you don't care" when people pick on you, because if people don't know what you're really thinking or feeling, they can't get to you.

8 Telling the plain truth all the time is boring. Most people exaggerate a bit when they are recounting something funny or exciting that has happened to them, because it makes a better story. It is more interesting and entertaining, and no-one is harmed by it. This is so common, there's a name for it. We call it 'embroidering the truth'.

Conclusion

There is no doubt that if you always tell the truth people will trust you and believe what you say. But if you want people to like you, it may be necessary sometimes to tell a 'little white lie'.

When in doubt, ask yourself these two questions:

➲ How would telling the truth about this make other people feel?

➲ How would it make me feel about myself?

It may be too simplistic to say you should always tell the truth but, nine times out of ten, you will probably still find that honesty is the best policy.

For and Against ... *Zoos*

Most of us have enjoyed a day at the zoo at some time, but a lot of people feel that keeping wild animals in captivity is wrong. They say that zoos are out of date now that we believe in animal rights. Zoo owners, on the other hand, say zoos have an important part to play in the preservation of animals under threat in the modern world.

Not many people still think it is all right to use wild animals in circuses. Is it time to think again about the arguments for and against zoos?

Conservation

The main argument for zoos is that many of them run breeding programmes to protect **endangered species**. Sometimes the offspring can be reintroduced into the wild. Even when this isn't possible, breeding in captivity means the species does not die out completely.

Not everybody agrees that breeding programmes are very useful. The biggest threat to animal species is from loss of **habitat**. As growing human populations clear forest areas for their own use animals lose their natural environment. Many **conservationists** believe we should be protecting natural environments rather than endangered species. They say that if you look after the habitat the animals can look after themselves.

Some people question the whole idea of protecting endangered species. Throughout history species have died out naturally as others became more successful. This is part of the process **Charles Darwin** called 'natural selection'. They say that trying to stop other species from dying out as mankind becomes more successful is going against nature.

Animal Rights

The main argument against zoos is that they take away the animals' right to freedom. Even though cages and enclosures are often bigger than they used to be, the animals are still not free.

Besides being enclosed, a zoo environment doesn't allow many animals to follow their natural instincts. **Carnivorous** animals fed on dead meat, for example, are not satisfying their instinct to hunt. Zoo animals often show signs of stress, boredom and anxiety.

On the other hand, animals in zoos enjoy a safe and comfortable environment, with adequate food and good veterinary care. You could say that zoos save animals from the sort of stresses they might suffer in the wild.

As for loss of freedom, some people think it's all right to keep animals in cages because they don't have feelings like human beings.

Education

Zoos give people the opportunity to see animals they would never normally have a chance to see. This, in itself, is educational. There are usually signs on each enclosure that give brief details about the animals, and most zoos also provide booklets and guides.

More recent developments include video presentations and **interactive computer games**. Some zoos also offer 'meet the animal' sessions, where visitors can touch and hold some of the less dangerous animals under the guidance of a keeper.

However, you could say that having television and computers means we no longer need to see animals in the flesh at all. We can learn about them in our own homes and classrooms. With modern film-making techniques, we can see animals in their natural environment, and that gives us a much better idea of what they are really like.

Entertainment

The reason most people go to zoos is not to support their conservation work or to find out about the animals – it's because zoos offer a great day out for people of all ages. Besides seeing the animals there are usually lots of other things to do. There are shops, cafeterias and picnic areas even in the smallest zoos. Some of the larger zoos have train rides, adventure playgrounds and amusement parks as well.

On the other hand, there are lots of other ways of having a great day out, and a great day out may not be a good enough reason for trapping and caging wild animals.

Conclusion

You can 'vote with your feet' on this issue. If you think zoos are a good idea, visit them. Your ticket money will help to pay for them to continue. If you think zoos are wrong, don't go. Zoos can only go on running as long as enough people support them.

Glossary

carnivorous animals Animals that eat meat.

conservationists People who think the natural environment should be protected for the animals and plants that live in it.

Darwin, Charles British scientist – born 1809, died1882. He put forward the theory of natural selection (see below).

designer labels Clothes that carry the logo of a famous clothing maker.

documentaries Programmes that report facts rather than telling stories.

endangered species Plant or animal species that are in danger of dying out completely. The three main causes are loss of habitat, hunting and pollution.

habitat A part of the natural environment where an animal usually lives.

interactive computer game A game where the display on the computer screen responds to instructions from the person playing it.

natural selection

The term used by Charles Darwin to describe the way that species adapt to changes in the environment. Only the individuals who are most able to adapt survive. Similarly, only the species which are most able to adapt survive.

soaps

Stories on radio or television about a group of people who live or work together. They have lots of episodes. The first soaps were on American radio in the 1930s. They were called 'soap operas' – 'soaps' for short – because they were sponsored by three big soap-making companies.

television

The world's first regular television broadcasting was by the BBC. It started in 1936. But very few people had their own television set until the 1950s.